This code revises the Acas Code of Prac
Duties and Activities which came into eff
code is issued under Section 199 of the
(Consolidation) Act 1992 and comes intc
State on 1 January 2010.

G000273018

1

Contents

Introduction

1. Under section 199 of the Trade Union and Labour Relations (Consolidation) Act 1992 the Advisory, Conciliation and Arbitration Service (Acas) has a duty to provide practical guidance on the time off to be permitted by an employer:

    (a) to a trade union official in accordance with section 168 of the Trade Union and Labour Relations (Consolidation) Act 1992; and

    (b) to a trade union member in accordance with section 170 of the Trade Union and Labour Relations (Consolidation) Act 1992.

    Section 199 of the Act, as amended by the Employment Act 2002, also provides for Acas to issue practical guidance on time off and training for Union Learning Representatives.

    This Code, which replaces the Code of Practice issued by Acas in 2003, is intended to provide such guidance. Advice on the role and responsibilities of employee representatives is provided in two Acas Guides: *Trade union representation in the workplace: a guide to managing time off, training and facilities* and *Non-union representation in the workplace: a guide to managing time off, training and facilities.*

Terminology

2. In this Code the term 'Trade union official', is replaced by 'union representative'. In practice there is often confusion between an 'official' and an 'officer' of a union and the term 'representative' is commonly used in practice. Section 119 of the Trade Union and Labour Relations (Consolidation) Act 1992 defines an official as '(a) an officer of the union or of a branch or section of the union, or (b) a person elected or appointed in accordance with the rules of the union to be a representative of its members or of some of them, and includes a person so elected or appointed who is an employee of the same employer as the members or one or more of the members whom he is to represent'. Section 181 (1) of the same Act defines a 'representative', for the purposes of sections 181 – 185 of the Act, as 'an official or other person authorised by the union to carry on such collective bargaining'.

In this Code a union representative means an employee who has been elected or appointed in accordance with the rules of the independent union to be a representative of all or some of the union's members in the particular company or workplace, or agreed group of workplaces where the union is recognised for collective bargaining purposes. This is intended to equate with the legal term 'trade union official' for the purposes of this Code.

The term 'union full-time officer' in this Code means a trade union official who is employed by an independent trade union to represent members in workplaces, or groups of workplaces, where the union is recognised for collective bargaining purposes.

A Union Learning Representative is an employee who is a member of an independent trade union recognised by the employer who has been elected or appointed in accordance with the rules of the union to be a learning representative of the union at the workplace.

The background

3. Union representatives have had a statutory right to reasonable paid time off from employment to carry out trade union duties and to undertake trade union training since the Employment Protection Act 1975. Union representatives and members were also given a statutory right to reasonable unpaid time off when taking part in trade union activities. Union duties must relate to matters covered by collective bargaining agreements between employers and trade unions and relate to the union representative's own employer, unless agreed otherwise in circumstances of multi-employer bargaining, and not, for example, to any associated employer. All the time off provisions were brought together in sections 168 – 170 of the Trade Union and Labour Relations (Consolidation) Act 1992. Section 43 of the Employment Act 2002 added a new right for Union Learning Representatives to take paid time off during working hours to undertake their duties and to undertake relevant training. The rights to time off for the purpose of carrying out trade union duties, and to take time off for training, were extended to union representatives engaged in duties related to redundancies under Section 188 of the amended 1992 Act and to duties relating to the Transfer of Undertakings (Protection of Employment) Regulations 2006.

General purpose of the Code

4. The general purpose of the statutory provisions and this Code of Practice is to aid and improve the effectiveness of relationships between employers and trade unions. Employers and unions have a joint responsibility to ensure that agreed arrangements work to mutual advantage by specifying how reasonable time off for union duties and activities and for training will work.

Structure of the Code

5. Section 1 of this Code provides guidance on time off for trade union duties. Section 2 deals with time off for training of trade union representatives and offers guidance on sufficient training for Union Learning Representatives. Section 3 considers time off for trade union activities. In each case the amount and frequency of time off, and the purposes for which and any conditions subject to which time off may be taken, are to be those that are reasonable in all the circumstances. Section 4 describes the responsibilities which employers and trade unions share in considering reasonable time off. Section 5 notes the advantages of reaching formal agreements on time off. Section 6 deals with industrial action and Section 7 with methods of appeal.

6. The annex to this Code reproduces the relevant statutory provisions on time off. To help differentiate between these and practical guidance, the summary of statutory provisions relating to time off which appears in the main text of the Code is in **bold type**. Practical guidance is in ordinary type. While every effort has been made to ensure that the summary of the statutory provisions included in this Code is accurate, only the courts can interpret the law authoritatively.

Status of the Code

7. **The provisions of this Code are admissible in evidence in proceedings before an Employment Tribunal relating to time off for trade union duties and activities. Any provisions of the Code which appear to the Tribunal to be relevant shall be taken into account. However, failure to observe any provision of the Code does not of itself render a person liable to any proceedings.**

Section 1

Time off For Trade Union Duties

Union representatives undertake a variety of roles in collective bargaining and in working with management, communicating with union members, liaising with their trade union and in handling individual disciplinary and grievance matters on behalf of employees. There are positive benefits for employers, employees and for union members in encouraging the efficient performance of union representatives' work, for example in aiding the resolution of problems and conflicts at work. The role can be both demanding and complex. In order to perform effectively union representatives need to have reasonable paid time off from their normal job in appropriate circumstances.

Entitlement

8.   **Employees who are union representatives of an independent trade union recognised by their employer are to be permitted reasonable time off during working hours to carry out certain trade union duties.**

9.   **Union representatives are entitled to time off where the duties are concerned with:**

   - **negotiations with the employer about matters which fall within section 178(2) of the Trade Union and Labour Relations (Consolidation) Act 1992 (TULR(C)A) and for which the union is recognised for the purposes of collective bargaining by the employer;**
   - **any other functions on behalf of employees of the employer which are related to matters falling within section 178(2) TULR(C)A and which the employer has agreed the union may perform;**
   - **the receipt of information from the employer and consultation by the employer under section 188 TULR(C)A, related to redundancy or under the Transfer of Undertakings (Protection of Employment) Regulations 2006 that applies to employees of the employer;**
   - **negotiations with a view to entering into an agreement under regulation 9 of the Transfer of Undertakings (Protection of Employment) Regulations 2006 that applies to employees of the employer; or**

- **the performance on behalf of employees of the employer of functions related to or connected with the making of an agreement under regulation 9 of the Transfer of Undertakings (Protection or Employment) Regulations 2006**.

Matters falling within section 178(2) TULR(C)A are listed in the sub headings of paragraph 13 below.

10. **The Safety Representatives and Safety Committees Regulations 1977 regulation 4(2)(a) requires that employers allow union health and safety representatives paid time, as is necessary, during working hours,to perform their functions.**

Further advice on time off provisions for health and safety representatives is provided by the Health and Safety Executive in their approved Code and Guidance 'Consulting workers on health and safety'. This is not covered in this Acas Code.

11. **An independent trade union is recognised by an employer when it is recognised to any extent for the purposes of collective bargaining. Where a trade union is not so recognised by an employer, employees have no statutory right to time off to undertake any duties except that of accompanying a worker at a disciplinary or grievance hearing** (see para 20).

Examples of trade union duties

12. **Subject to the recognition or other agreement, trade union representatives should be allowed to take reasonable time off for duties concerned with negotiations or, where their employer has agreed, for duties concerned with other functions related to or connected with the subjects of collective bargaining.**

13. **The subjects connected with collective bargaining may include one or more of the following:**

   (a) **terms and conditions of employment, or the physical conditions in which workers are required to work.** Examples could include:
   - pay
   - hours of work
   - holidays and holiday pay
   - sick pay arrangements

- pensions
- learning and training
- equality and diversity
- notice periods
- the working environment
- operation of digital equipment and other machinery;

(b) **engagement or non engagement, or termination or suspension of employment or the duties of employment, of one or more workers.** Examples could include:
- recruitment and selection policies
- human resource planning
- redundancy and dismissal arrangements;

(c) **allocation of work or the duties of employment as between workers or groups of workers.** Examples could include:
- job grading
- job evaluation
- job descriptions
- flexible working practices
- work-life balance;

(d) **matters of discipline.** Examples could include:
- disciplinary procedures
- arrangements for representing or accompanying employees at internal interviews
- arrangements for appearing on behalf of trade union members, or as witnesses, before agreed outside appeal bodies or employment tribunals;

(e) **trade union membership or non membership.** Examples could include:
- representational arrangements
- any union involvement in the induction of new workers;

(f) **facilities for trade union representatives.** Examples could include any agreed arrangements for the provision of:
- accommodation
- equipment
- names of new workers to the union;

(g) **machinery for negotiation or consultation and other procedures.** Examples could include arrangements for:
- collective bargaining at the employer and/or multi-employer level
- grievance procedures
- joint consultation
- communicating with members
- communicating with other union representatives and union full-time officers concerned with collective bargaining with the employer.

14. The duties of a representative of a recognised trade union must be connected with or related to negotiations or the performance of functions both in time and subject matter. Reasonable time off may be sought, for example, to:
- prepare for negotiations, including attending relevant meetings
- inform members of progress and outcomes
- prepare for meetings with the employer about matters for which the trade union has only representational rights.

15. **Trade union duties will also be related to the receipt of information and consultation related to the handling of collective redundancies where an employer is proposing to dismiss as redundant 20 or more employees at one establishment within a period of 90 days, and where the Transfer of Undertakings (Protection of Employees) Regulations apply but also including the negotiations with a view to entering an agreement under regulation 9 of the Regulations (variation of contract in insolvency).**

Union Learning Representatives

16. **Employees who are members of an independent trade union recognised by the employer can take reasonable time off to undertake the duties of a Union Learning Representative, provided that the union has given the employer notice in writing that the employee is a learning representative of the trade union and the training condition is met** (see paras 28 – 33 for further information on the training condition) **The functions for which time off as a Union Learning Representative is allowed are:**
- **analysing learning or training needs**

- **providing information and advice about learning or training matters**
- **arranging learning or training**
- **promoting the value of learning or training**
- **consulting the employer about carrying on any such activities**
- **preparation to carry out any of the above activities**
- **undergoing relevant training.**

In practice, the roles and responsibilities of Union Learning Representatives will often vary by union and by workplace but must include one or more of these functions. In some cases it may be helpful if Union Learning Representatives attend meetings concerned with agreeing and promoting learning agreements. Employers may also see it in their interests to grant paid time off for these representatives to attend meetings with external partners concerned with the development and provision of workforce training.

Recognition needs to be given to the varying roles of Union Learning Representatives where the post holder also undertakes additional duties as a union representative.

17. Many employers have in place well established training and development programmes for their employees. Union Learning Representatives should liaise with their employers to ensure that their respective training activities complement one another and that the scope for duplication is minimised.

Payment for time off for trade union duties

18. **An employer who permits union representatives time off for trade union duties must pay them for the time off taken. The employer must pay either the amount that the union representative would have earned had they worked during the time off taken or, where earnings vary with the work done, an amount calculated by reference to the average hourly earnings for the work they are employed to do.**

The calculation of pay for the time taken for trade union duties should be undertaken with due regard to the type of payment system applying to the union representative including, as appropriate, shift premia, performance related pay, bonuses and commission earnings. Where pay is linked to the achievement of performance targets it may be necessary to adjust such targets to take account of the reduced time the representative has to achieve the desired performance.

19. **There is no statutory requirement to pay for time off where the duty is carried out at a time when the union representative would not otherwise have been at work unless the union representative works flexible hours, such as night shift, but needs to perform representative duties during normal hours. Staff who work part time will be entitled to be paid if staff who work full time would be entitled to be paid. In all cases the amount of time off must be reasonable.**

Time off to Accompany Workers at Disciplinary or Grievance Hearings

20. **Trade union representatives are statutorily entitled to take a reasonable amount of paid time off to accompany a worker at a disciplinary or grievance hearing so long as they have been certified by their union as being capable of acting as a worker's companion. The right to time off in these situations applies regardless of whether the certified person belongs to a recognised union or not although the worker being accompanied must be employed by the same employer.** Time off for a union representative or a certified person to accompany a worker of another employer is a matter for voluntary agreement between the parties concerned.

Section 2

Training of union representatives in aspects of employment relations and employee development

Training is important for union representatives to enable them to carry out their duties effectively. Training should be available both to newly appointed and to more established union representatives. It is desirable, from time to time where resources permit it, for joint training and development activities between union representatives and managers to occur.

Entitlement

21. **Employees who are union representatives of an independent trade union recognised by their employer are to be permitted reasonable time off during working hours to undergo training in aspects of industrial relations relevant to the carrying out of their trade union duties. These duties must be concerned with:**

    - **negotiations with the employer about matters which fall within section 178(2) TULR(C)A and for which the union is recognised to any extent for the purposes of collective bargaining by the employer; or**
    - **any other functions on behalf of employees of the employer which are related to matters falling within section 178(2) TULR(C)A and which the employer has agreed the union may perform;**
    - **matters associated with information and consultation concerning collective redundancy and the Transfer of Undertakings, and the negotiation of an agreement under Regulation 9 of the Transfer of Undertakings (Protection of Employees) Regulations.**

    Matters falling within section 178(2) TULR(C)A are set out in paragraph 13 above.

22. **The Safety Representatives and Safety Committees Regulations 1977 regulation 4(2)(b) requires that employers allow union health and safety representatives to undergo training in aspects of their functions that is 'reasonable in all the circumstances'.**

Further advice on the training of health and safety representatives is provided by the Health and Safety Executive in their approved Code and Guidance 'Consulting workers on health and safety'. This is not covered in this Acas Code.

23. **Employees who are Trade Union Learning Representatives are also permitted reasonable time off during working hours to undergo training relevant to their functions as a Union Learning Representative.**

What is relevant employment relations training?

24. **Training should be in aspects of employment relations relevant to the duties of a union representative.** There is no one recommended syllabus for training as a union representative's duties will vary according to:
    - the collective bargaining arrangements at the place of work, particularly the scope of the recognition or other agreement
    - the structure of the union
    - the role of the union representative
    - the handling of proposed collective redundancies or the transfer of undertakings.

25. **The training must also be approved by the Trades Union Congress or by the independent trade union of which the employee is a union representative.**

26. Union representatives are more likely to carry out their duties effectively if they possess skills and knowledge relevant to their duties. In particular, employers should be prepared to consider releasing union representatives for initial training in basic representational skills as soon as possible after their election or appointment, bearing in mind that suitable courses may be infrequent. Reasonable time off could also be considered, for example:

- for training courses to develop the union representative's skills in representation, accompaniment, negotiation and consultation
- for further training particularly where the union representative has special responsibilities, for example in collective redundancy and transfer of undertakings circumstances
- for training courses to familiarise or update union representatives on issues reflecting the developing needs of the workforce they represent
- for training where there are proposals to change the structure and topics of negotiation about matters for which the union is recognised; or where significant changes in the organisation of work are being contemplated
- for training where legal change may affect the conduct of employment relations at the place of work and may require the reconsideration of existing agreements
- for training where a union representative undertakes the role of accompanying employees in grievance and disciplinary hearings.

27. E-learning tools, related to the role of union representatives, should be used where available and appropriate. However, their best use is as an additional learning aid rather than as a replacement to attendance at approved trade union and Trades Union Congress training courses. Time needs to be given during normal working hours for union representatives to take advantage of e-learning where it is available.

Training For Union Learning Representatives

28. **Employees who are members of an independent trade union recognised by the employer are entitled to reasonable paid time off to undertake the functions of a Union Learning Representative. To qualify for paid time off the member must be sufficiently trained to carry out duties as a learning representative:**
    - **either at the time when their trade union gives notice to their employer in writing that they are a learning representative of the trade union**
    - **or within six months of that date.**

29. **In the latter case, the trade union is required to give the employer notice in writing that the employee will be undergoing such training and when the employee has done so to give the employer notice of that fact. During the six month period in which he or she is undergoing this training, the Union Learning Representative must be allowed time off to perform their duties.** It should be confirmed by the union in a letter that the training undertaken is sufficient to allow the Learning Representative to undertake their role and it is good practice for the union to give details of the training which has been completed and any previous training that has been taken into account. In the interests of good practice, the six month qualifying period may be extended, with agreement, to take into account any significant unforeseen circumstances such as prolonged absence from work due to ill health, pregnancy, bereavement or unavoidable delays in arranging an appropriate training course.

30. To satisfy this training requirement an employee will need to be able to demonstrate to their trade union that they have received sufficient training to enable them to operate competently in one or more of the following areas of activity relevant to their duties as a Union Learning Representative:

analysing learning or training needs;

- this could for example include understanding the different methods for identifying learning interests or needs, being able to effectively identify and record individual learning needs or being able to draw up a plan to meet identified learning requirements.

providing information and advice about learning or training matters;

- including, for example, the development of communication and interviewing skills
- knowledge of available opportunities, in order to be able to provide accurate information to members about learning opportunities within and outside the workplace
- the ability to signpost members to other sources of advice and guidance where additional support is needed, for example, basic skills tutors or fuller in depth professional career guidance.

arranging and supporting learning and training;
- for example, obtaining and providing information on learning opportunities including e-learning where available, supporting and encouraging members to access learning opportunities and helping to develop and improve local learning opportunities;

promoting the value of learning and training;
- some examples of this activity could be, understanding current initiatives for the development of learning and skills in the workplace, promoting the value of learning to members and within trade union networks and structures, working with employers to meet the learning and skill needs of both individuals and the organisation, and appreciating the value of learning agreements and how they may be developed.

31. An employee could demonstrate to their trade union that they have received sufficient training to enable them to operate competently in one or more of these areas of activity by:
- completing a training course approved by the Trades Union Congress or by the independent trade union of which the employee is a Union Learning Representative, or by
- showing that they have previously gained the relevant expertise and experience to operate effectively as a learning representative.

In the latter case, previous experience and expertise gained in areas such as teaching, training, counselling, providing careers advice and guidance or human resource development, may well be relevant, as may periods of extensive on-the-job training and experience gained in shadowing an experienced Union Learning Representative.

32. Reasonable time off should also be considered for further training to help Union Learning Representatives develop their skills and competencies.

33. Although not required by law it is recognised that there would be clear advantages both to the individual and the organisation if training undertaken leads to a recognised qualification standard.

Payment for time off for training

34. **An employer who permits union representatives or Union Learning Representatives time off to attend relevant training, must pay them for the time off taken. The employer must pay either the amount that the union representative or the Union Learning Representative would have earned had they worked during the time off taken or, where earnings vary with the work done, an amount calculated by reference to the average hourly earnings for the work they are employed to do.**

   The calculation of pay for the time taken for training should be undertaken with due regard to the type of payment system applying to the union representative and Union Learning Representative including, as appropriate, shift premia, performance related pay, bonuses and commission earnings. Where pay is linked to the achievement of performance targets it may be necessary to adjust such targets to take account of the reduced time the representative has to achieve the desired performance.

35. **There is no statutory requirement to pay for time off where training is undertaken at a time when the union representative or Union Learning Representative would not otherwise have been at work unless the union representative or Union Learning Representative works flexible hours, such as night shift, but needs to undertake training during normal hours. Staff who work part time will be entitled to be paid if staff who work full time would be entitled to be paid. In all cases, the amount of time off must be reasonable.**

Section 3

Time off for trade union activities

To operate effectively and democratically, trade unions need the active participation of members. It can also be very much in employers' interests that such participation is assured and help is given to promote effective communication between union representatives and members in the workplace.

Entitlement

36. **An employee who is a member of an independent trade union recognised by the employer in respect of that description of employee is to be permitted reasonable time off during working hours to take part in any trade union activity. An employee who is a member of an independent and recognised trade union is also permitted to take reasonable time off during working hours for the purposes of accessing the services of a Union Learning Representative (provided those services are services for which the Union Learning Representative is entitled to time off).**

What are examples of trade union activities?

37. The activities of a <u>trade union member</u> can be, for example:
   - attending workplace meetings to discuss and vote on the outcome of negotiations with the employer. Where relevant, and with the employer's agreement, this can include attending such workplace meetings at the employer's neighbouring locations.
   - meeting full time officers to discuss issues relevant to the workplace
   - voting in union elections
   - having access to services provided by a Union Learning representative.

38. Where the member is acting as a representative of a recognised union, activities can be, for example, taking part in:

- branch, area or regional meetings of the union where the business of the union is under discussion
- meetings of official policy making bodies such as the executive committee or annual conference
- meetings with full time officers to discuss issues relevant to the workplace.

39. **There is no right to time off for trade union activities which themselves consist of industrial action.**

Payment for time off for trade union activities

40. Paragraphs 18 and 19 set out the statutory entitlement to payment for time off to undertake trade union <u>duties</u>.

41. **There is no statutory requirement that union members or representatives be paid for time off taken on trade union <u>activities</u>.** Nevertheless employers may want to consider payment in certain circumstances, for example to ensure that workplace meetings are fully representative or to ensure that employees have access to services provided by Union Learning Representatives.

Section 4

The responsibilities of employers and trade unions

Employers, trade unions, union representatives and line managers should work together to ensure that time off provisions, including training, operate effectively and for mutual benefit. Union representatives need to be able to communicate with management, each other, their trade union and employees. To do so they need to be able to use appropriate communication media and other facilities.

General considerations

42. **The amount and frequency of time off should be reasonable in all the circumstances.** Although the statutory provisions apply to all employers without exception as to size and type of business or service, trade unions should be aware of the wide variety of difficulties and operational requirements to be taken into account when seeking or agreeing arrangements for time off, for example:
    • the size of the organisation and the number of workers
    • the production process
    • the need to maintain a service to the public
    • the need for safety and security at all times.

43. Employers in turn should have in mind the difficulties for trade union representatives and members in ensuring effective representation and communications with, for example:
    • shift workers
    • part-time workers
    • home workers
    • teleworkers or workers not working in a fixed location
    • those employed at dispersed locations
    • workers with particular domestic commitments including those on leave for reasons of maternity, paternity or care responsibilities
    • workers with special needs such as disabilities or language requirements.

44. For time off arrangements to work satisfactorily trade unions should:
    - ensure that union representatives are aware of their role, responsibilities and functions
    - inform management, in writing, as soon as possible of appointments or resignations of union representatives
    - ensure that union representatives receive any appropriate written credentials promptly
    - ensure that employers receive details of the functions of union representatives where they carry out special duties or functions.

45. Employers should ensure that, where necessary, work cover and/or work load reductions are provided when time off is required. This can include the allocation of duties to other employees, rearranging work to a different time or a reduction in workloads.

46. While there is no statutory right for facilities for union representatives, except for representatives engaged in duties related to collective redundancies and the Transfer of Undertakings, employers should, where practical, make available to union representatives the facilities necessary for them to perform their duties efficiently and communicate effectively with their members, colleague union representatives and full-time officers. Where resources permit the facilities should include:
    - accommodation for meetings which could include provision for Union Learning Representatives and a union member(s) to meet to discuss relevant training matters
    - access to a telephone and other communication media used or permitted in the workplace such as email, intranet and internet
    - the use of noticeboards
    - where the volume of the union representative's work justifies it, the use of dedicated office space
    - confidential space where an employee involved in a grievance or disciplinary matter can meet their representative or to discuss other confidential matters
    - access to members who work at a different location
    - access to e-learning tools where computer facilities are available.

47. When using facilities provided by the employer for the purposes of communication with their members or their trade union, union representatives must comply with agreed procedures both in respect of the use of such facilities and also in respect of access to and use of company information. The agreed procedures will be either those agreed between the union and the employer as part of an agreement on time off (see section 6) or comply with general rules applied to all employees in the organisation. In particular, union representatives must respect and maintain the confidentiality of information they are given access to where, the disclosure would seriously harm the functioning of, or would be prejudicial to, the employer's business interests. The disclosure of information for collective bargaining purposes is covered by the Acas Code of Practice on that topic. Union representatives should understand that unauthorised publication risks damaging the employer's business, straining relations with the representative body concerned, possible breaches of individual contracts of employment and, in extreme cases such as unauthorised publication of price-sensitive information, the commission of criminal offences.

48. Union representatives will have legitimate expectations that they and their members are entitled to communicate without intrusion in the form of monitoring by their employer. Rules concerning the confidentiality of communications involving union representatives should be agreed between the employer and the union. Guidance on this is set out in paragraphs 49 and 57 below.

49. Employers must respect the confidential and sensitive nature of communications between union representatives and their members and trade union. They should not normally carry out regular or random monitoring of union emails. Only in exceptional circumstances may employers require access to communications but such access should be subject to the general rules set out in statute and the Employment Practices Code issued by the Information Commissioner's Office. In the context of the Data Protection Act 1998 whether a person is a member of a trade union or not is defined as sensitive personal data. This also applies to data concerning individuals, for example communications concerned with possible or actual grievance and disciplinary issues. There are therefore very strict provisions on how such data can be used and monitored in compliance with the law.

Requesting time off

50. Trade union representatives and members requesting time off to pursue their duties or activities or to access the services of a Union Learning Representative should provide management, especially their line manager, with as much notice as practically possible concerning:
    - the purpose of such time off, while preserving personal confidential information relating to individuals in grievance or disciplinary matters
    - the intended location
    - the timing and duration of time off required.

51. Union representatives should minimise business disruption by being prepared to be as flexible as possible in seeking time off in circumstances where the immediate or unexpected needs of the business make it difficult for colleagues or managers to provide cover for them in their absence. Equally employers should recognise the mutual obligation to allow union representatives to undertake their duties.

52. In addition, union representatives who request paid time off to undergo relevant training should:
    - give at least a few weeks' notice to management of nominations for training courses
    - provide details of the contents of the training course.

53. When deciding whether requests for paid time off should be granted, consideration would need to be given as to their reasonableness, for example to ensure adequate cover for safety or to safeguard the production process or the provision of service. Consideration should also be given to allowing Union Learning Representatives access to a room in which they can discuss training in a confidential manner with an employee. Similarly, managers and unions should seek to agree a mutually convenient time which minimises the effect on production or services. Where workplace meetings are requested, consideration should be given to holding them, for example:
    - towards the end of a shift or the working week
    - before or after a meal break.

54. For their part line managers should be familiar with the rights and duties of union representatives regarding time off. They should be encouraged to take reasonable steps as necessary in the planning and management of representatives' time off and the provision of cover or work load reduction, taking into account the legitimate needs of such union representatives to discharge their functions and receive training efficiently and effectively.

55. Employers need to consider each application for time off on its merits; they should also consider the reasonableness of the request in relation to agreed time off already taken or in prospect.

Section 5

Agreements on time off

To take account of the wide variety of circumstances and problems which can arise, there can be positive advantages for employers and trade unions in establishing agreements on time off in ways that reflect their own situations. It should be borne in mind, however, that the absence of a formal agreement on time off does not in itself deny an individual any statutory entitlement. Nor does any agreement supersede statutory entitlement to time off.

56. A formal agreement can help to:
    - provide clear guidelines against which applications for time off can be determined
    - establish realistic expectations on the part of union representatives and managers
    - avoid misunderstanding
    - facilitate better planning
    - ensure fair and reasonable treatment.

57. Agreements should specify:
    - the amount of time off permitted recognising that this will vary according the fluctuations in demand on the union representatives' role
    - the occasions on which time off can be taken including meetings with management, meetings with other union representatives, time needed to prepare for meetings, communicating with members and their trade union, time to undertake e-learning if appropriate and to attend approved training events
    - in what circumstances time off will be paid
    - arrangements for taking time off at short notice
    - how pay is to be calculated
    - to whom time off will be paid
    - the facilities and equipment to be provided and limits to their use, if any

- arrangements for ensuring confidentiality of communications involving union representatives. These should include agreed rules on the use of data and the exceptional cases where monitoring may be necessary, for example in cases of suspected illegal use, specifying the circumstances where such monitoring may be undertaken and the means by which it is to be done, for example by company IT or security personnel
- the role of line managers in granting permission to legitimate requests for time off and, where appropriate and practical, ensuring that adequate cover or work load reductions are provided
- the procedure for requesting time off
- the procedure for resolving grievances about time off.

58. In addition, it would be sensible for agreements to make clear:
    - arrangements for the appropriate payment to be made when time off relates in part to union duties and in part to union activities
    - how and in what circumstances payment might be made to shift and part time employees undertaking trade union duties outside their normal working hours.

59. Agreements for time off and other facilities for union representation should be consistent with wider agreements which deal with such matters as constituencies, number of representatives and the election of officials.

60. The operation of time off agreements or arrangements should be jointly reviewed by the parties from time to time.

61. In smaller organisations, it might be thought more appropriate for employers and unions to reach understandings about how requests for time off are to be made; and more broadly to agree flexible arrangements which can accommodate their particular circumstances.

Section 6

Industrial action

62. Employers and unions have a responsibility to use agreed procedures to settle problems and avoid industrial action. Time off may therefore be permitted for this purpose particularly where there is a dispute. **There is no right to time off for trade union activities which themselves consist of industrial action.** However, where a union representative is not taking part in industrial action but represents members involved, normal arrangements for time off with pay for the union representatives should apply.

Section 7

Resolving disputes

There is advantage in agreeing ways in which disputes concerning time off arrangements, including training and access to facilities, can be settled and any appropriate procedures to resolve disputes should be followed.

63. Every effort should be made to resolve any dispute or grievance in relation to time off work for union duties or activities. **Where the grievance remains unresolved, union representatives, Union Learning Representatives or members have a right to complain to an employment tribunal that their employer has failed to allow reasonable time off or, in the case of a Union Learning Representative or union representative, has failed to pay for all or part of the time off taken. Such complaints may be resolved by conciliation by Acas or through a compromise agreement and, if this is successful, no tribunal hearing will be necessary.** Acas assistance may also be sought without the need for a formal complaint to a tribunal.

Annex – The law on time off for trade union duties and activities

Section 168 of the Trade Union and Labour Relations (Consolidation) Act 1992, states:

(1)   An employer shall permit an employee of his who is an official of an independent trade union recognised by the employer to take time off during his working hours for the purpose of carrying out any duties of his, as such an official, concerned with –

(a)   negotiations with the employer related to or connected with matters falling within section 178(2) (collective bargaining) in relation to which the trade union is recognised by the employer, or

(b)   the performance on behalf of employees of the employer of functions related to or connected with matters falling within that provision which the employer has agreed may be so performed by the trade union, or

(c)   receipt of information from the employer and consultation by the employer under section 188 (redundancies) or under the Transfer of Undertakings (Protection of Employment) Regulations 2006, or

(d)   negotiations with a view to entering into an agreement under regulation 9 of the Transfer of Undertakings (Protection of Employment) Regulations 2006 that applies to employees of the employer, or

(e)   the performance on behalf of employees of the employer of functions related to or connected with the making of an agreement under that regulation.

(2)   He shall also permit such an employee to take time off during his working hours for the purpose of undergoing training in aspects of industrial relations –

(a)   relevant to the carrying out of such duties as are mentioned in subsection (1), and

(b)   approved by the Trades Union Congress or by the independent trade union of which he is an official.

(3) The amount of time off which an employee is to be permitted to take under this section and the purposes for which, the occasions on which and any conditions subject to which time off may be so taken are those that are reasonable in all the circumstances having regard to any relevant provisions of a Code of Practice issued by ACAS.

(4) An employee may present a complaint to an employment tribunal that his employer has failed to permit him to take time off as required by this section.

Section 168A of the Trade Union and Labour Relations (Consolidation) Act 1992 states

(1) An employer shall permit an employee of his who is –
    (a) a member of an independent trade union recognised by the employer, and
    (b) a learning representative of the trade union,

to take time off during his working hours for any of the following purposes.

(2) The purposes are –
    (a) carrying on any of the following activities in relation to qualifying members of the trade union-
        (i) analysing learning or training needs,
        (ii) providing information and advice about learning or training matters,
        (iii) arranging learning or training, and
        (iv) promoting the value of learning or training,

    (b) consulting the employer about carrying on any such activities in relation to such members of the trade union,

    (c) preparing for any of the things mentioned in paragraphs (a) and (b).

(3) Subsection (1) only applies if –
    (a) the trade union has given the employer notice in writing that the employee is a learning representative of the trade union, and
    (b) the training condition is met in relation to him.

(4)   The training condition is met if –

(a)   the employee has undergone sufficient training to enable him to carry on the activities mentioned in subsection (2), and the trade union has given the employer notice in writing of that fact,

(b)   the trade union has in the last six months given the employer notice in writing that the employee will be undergoing such training, or

(c)   within six months of the trade union giving the employer notice in writing that the employee will be undergoing such training, the employee has done so, and the trade union has given the employer notice of that fact.

(5)   Only one notice under subsection (4)(b) may be given in respect of any one employee.

(6)   References in subsection (4) to sufficient training to carry out the activities mentioned in subsection (2) are to training that is sufficient for those purposes having regard to any relevant provision of a Code of Practice issued by ACAS or the Secretary of State.

(7)   If an employer is required to permit an employee to take time off under subsection (1), he shall also permit the employee to take time off during his working hours for the following purposes –

(a)   undergoing training which is relevant to his functions as a learning representative, and

(b)   where the trade union has in the last six months given the employer notice under subsection (4)(b) in relation to the employee, undergoing such training as is mentioned in subsection (4)(a).

(8)   The amount of time off which an employee is to be permitted to take under this section and the purposes for which, the occasions on which and any conditions subject to which time off may be so taken are those that are reasonable in all the circumstances having regard to any relevant provision of a Code of Practice issued by ACAS or the Secretary of State.

(9)   An employee may present a complaint to an employment tribunal that his employer has failed to permit him to take time off as required by this section.

(10) In subsection (2)(a), the reference to qualifying members of the trade union is to members of the trade union –

    (a) who are employees of the employer of a description in respect of which the union is recognised by the employer, and

    (b) in relation to whom it is the function of the union learning representative to act as such.

(11) For the purposes of this section, a person is a learning representative of a trade union if he is appointed or elected as such in accordance with its rules.

Section 169 of the Trade Union and Labour Relations (Consolidation) Act 1992 states:

(1)   An employer who permits an employee to take time off under section 168 or 168A shall pay him for the time taken off pursuant to the permission.

(2)   Where the employee's remuneration for the work he would ordinarily have been doing during that time does not vary with the amount of work done, he shall be paid as if he had worked at that work for the whole of that time.

(3)   Where the employee's remuneration for the work he would ordinarily have been doing during that time varies with the amount of work done, he shall be paid an amount calculated by reference to the average hourly earnings for that work.
The average hourly earnings shall be those of the employee concerned or, if no fair estimate can be made of those earnings, the average hourly earnings for work of that description of persons in comparable employment with the same employer or, if there are no such persons, a figure of average hourly earnings which is reasonable in the circumstances.

(4)   A right to be paid an amount under this section does not affect any right of an employee in relation to remuneration under his contract of employment, but –

    (a) any contractual remuneration paid to an employee in respect of a period of time off to which this section applies shall go towards discharging any liability of the employer under this section in respect of that period, and

(b) any payment under this section in respect of a period shall go towards discharging any liability of the employer to pay contractual remuneration in respect of that period.

(5) An employee may present a complaint to an employment tribunal that his employer has failed to pay him in accordance with this section.

Section 170 of the Trade Union and Labour Relations (Consolidation) Act 1992 states:

(1) An employer shall permit an employee of his who is a member of an independent trade union recognised by the employer in respect of that description of employee to take time off during his working hours for the purpose of taking part in –
(a) any activities of the union, and
(b) any activities in relation to which the employee is acting as a representative of the union.

(2) The right conferred by subsection (1) does not extend to activities which themselves consist of industrial action, whether or not in contemplation or furtherance of a trade dispute.

(2A) The right conferred by subsection (1) does not extend to time off for the purpose of acting as, or having access to services provided by, a learning representative of a trade union.

(2B) An employer shall permit an employee of his who is a member of an independent trade union recognised by the employer in respect of that description of employee to take time off during his working hours for the purpose of having access to services provided by a person in his capacity as a learning representative of the trade union.

(2C) Subsection (2B) only applies if the learning representative would be entitled to time off under subsection (1) of section 168A for the purpose of carrying on in relation to the employee activities of the kind mentioned in subsection (2) of that section.

(3) The amount of time off which an employee is to be permitted to take under this section and the purposes for which, the occasions on which and any conditions subject to which time off may be so taken are those that are reasonable in all the circumstances having regard to any relevant provisions of a Code of Practice issued by ACAS.

(4) An employee may present a complaint to an employment tribunal that his employer has failed to permit him to take time off as required by this section.

(5) For the purposes of this section –
  (a) a person is a learning representative of a trade union if he is appointed or elected as such in accordance with its rules, and
  (b) a person who is a learning representative of a trade union acts as such if he carries on the activities mentioned in section 168A(2) in that capacity.

Section 178(1) – (3) of the Trade Union and Labour Relations (Consolidation) Act 1992, states:

(1) In this Act "collective agreement" means any agreement or arrangement made by or on behalf of one or more trade unions and one or more employers or employers' associations and relating to one or more of the matters specified below; and "collective bargaining" means negotiations relating to or connected with one or more of those matters.

(2) The matters referred to above are –
  (a) terms and conditions of employment, or the physical conditions in which any workers are required to work;
  (b) engagement or non engagement, or termination or suspension of employment or the duties of employment, of one or more workers;
  (c) allocation of work or the duties of employment as between workers or groups of workers;
  (d) matters of discipline;
  (e) a worker's membership or non membership of a trade union;
  (f) facilities for officials of trade unions; and
  (g) machinery for negotiation or consultation, and other procedures, relating to any of the above matters, including the recognition by employers or employers' associations of the right of a trade union to represent workers in such negotiation or consultation or in the carrying out of such procedures.

(3)   In this Act "recognition", in relation to a trade union, means the recognition of the union by an employer, or two or more associated employers, to any extent, for the purpose of collective bargaining; and "recognised" and other related expressions shall be construed accordingly.

Section 173(1) of the Trade Union and Labour Relations (Consolidation) Act 1992, states:

For the purposes of sections 168, 168A and 170 the working hours of an employee shall be taken to be any time when in accordance with his contract of employment he is required to be at work.

Section 119 of the Trade Union and Labour Relations (Consolidation) Act 1992 states:

"official" means –

(a)   an officer of the union or of a branch or section of the union, or

(b)   a person elected or appointed in accordance with the rules of the union to be a representative of its members or of some of them,

and includes a person so elected or appointed who is an employee of the same employer as the members or one or more of the members whom he is to represent.